D1320397

NEW FRANCE AND THE FUR TRADE

Douglas Baldwin

Weigl

CALGARY
www.weigl.com

We acknowledge the financial support of the Government of Canada through the Book Publishing Industry Development Program (BPIDP) for our publishing activities.

Published by Weigl Educational Publishers Limited
6325 – 10 Street SE
Calgary, Alberta, Canada
T2H 2Z9

Web site: www.weigl.com

National Library of Canada Cataloguing-in-Publication Data

Baldwin, Douglas, 1944-
    New France and the fur trade / Douglas Baldwin.

(Canadian history)
Includes bibliographical references and index.
For use in grades 6-8.
ISBN 1-55388-011-0

    1. Canada--History--To 1763 (New France)--Juvenile literature. 2. Fur trade--Canada--History--Juvenile literature.
I. Title. II. Series: Canadian history (Calgary, Alta.)

FC305.B34 2002   971.01   C2002-901453-0
F1030.B34 2002

Printed in the United States of America
1 2 3 4 5 6 7 8 9 0   06 05 04 03 02

Project Coordinator
Michael Lowry
Editor
Lynn Hamilton
Copy Editor
Nicole Bezic King
Photo Researcher
Gayle Murdoff
Designer
Warren Clark
Layout
Terry Paulhus

CONTENTS

EUROPEAN Interest in North America

Conflicts between the French, English, and Aboriginal peoples arose because of competition for land and control of the fur trade.

In the 1400s, European countries tried to find new water routes to Asia. They wanted to trade for spices, silks, and jewels found in the countries there. New instruments were invented to guide sailors on long sea voyages. Better sailing ships were built with more space for supplies and crew. Many explorers thought that they could find a route to Asia by sailing west across the Atlantic Ocean.

Expeditions from Portugal, Spain, France, and England led to the exploration of the Americas. When explorers reached North America, they met Aboriginal peoples who taught them about their environment and guided them on their trips. The explorers did not find silks or spices in North America, but the Europeans learned that North America was rich in other resources. Fishers from England, France, Spain, Portugal, and Holland came each spring to fish for cod in the Grand Banks of Newfoundland, the Gulf of St. Lawrence, and the Bay of Fundy.

Even though North America was the home of many Aboriginal peoples, European countries competed with one another to claim land there. By establishing colonies in what is now Canada, the European powers hoped to increase their power and wealth.

Aboriginal peoples participated in the fur trade in exchange for European goods. Conflicts between the French, the English, and Aboriginal groups arose as a result of the fur trade. Despite many challenges, France was eventually able to establish colonies in what became known as New France.

The First Settlements

Samuel de Champlain was a French explorer and mapmaker. He made his first trip to Canada in 1603 on a ship captained by François Gravé Du Pont. Champlain made many of the first drawings and maps of the new land. He wrote descriptions of the people he met on his travels, and of the places he explored around the St. Lawrence River. He was one of the first Europeans to set up trading posts and settlements in early Canada. Because of his many contributions, he is known as the "Father of New France."

FURTHER UNDERSTANDING

New France New France was a **colony** in present-day Canada. The colony occupied territory around the St. Lawrence River that was claimed by France in the 1600s.

Port-Royal Samuel de Champlain's colony survived from 1605 to 1607, when it was abandoned. It was later revived by Biencourt de Poutrincourt in 1610, but was destroyed by the English in 1613. Other settlements were founded in the area, but none were permanent. The site has been reconstructed as Port-Royal National Historical Site, and is located outside of Annapolis Royal, Nova Scotia.

Champlain returned to France and told King Henry IV about the potential for settlement and a profitable fur trade in North America. He learned that King Henry IV had granted a fur trade **monopoly** to Pierre Du Gua de Monts for ten years. This gave de Monts the exclusive right to trade with Aboriginal peoples. In return, de Monts was expected to explore the land, establish a colony, and convert Aboriginal peoples to **Christianity**.

In 1604, Champlain travelled to New France with de Monts and about eighty other people to start a fur-trading post. They explored the Bay of Fundy area and finally chose an island in the mouth of the Ste-Croix River for their settlement. It appeared to be a location that would be easy to defend and had resources such as lumber and shellfish. After a hard winter, they learned that this was a poor location. There was no fresh water, and the land was unsuitable for agriculture.

The settlers moved across the bay to the mainland and built a settlement called Port-Royal. As a result of illegal fur trading, the colony was having trouble maintaining its monopoly. When the king cancelled the monopoly, Champlain returned to France, but he longed to return to North America.

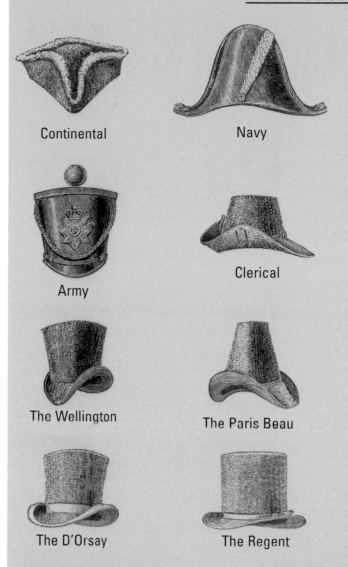

Continental

Navy

Army

Clerical

The Wellington

The Paris Beau

The D'Orsay

The Regent

■ Beaver was once considered to be the most valuable fur. Felt hats made from the underfur of the beaver pelt were symbols of prestige.

■ Samuel de Champlain was one of the first European explorers to establish fur trading posts along the St. Lawrence River. He encouraged the Algonquin and Montagnais living in the region to trade beaver pelts in exchange for European goods.

The Father of New FRANCE

Champlain chose a spot along the river that could be easily defended by cannons.

De Monts convinced King Henry IV to grant him another fur-trade monopoly, this time for a period of one year. In exchange, he was expected to establish a colony along the St. Lawrence River. In 1608, working with de Monts' company, Champlain agreed to make another trip to North America. De Monts placed Champlain in charge of an expedition to the St. Lawrence River region. Champlain's goal was to start a trading post that would help France protect its monopoly of the region's fur trade. He chose a spot along the river that was protected by cliffs, because it could be easily defended by cannons. It was the former site of Stadacona. Champlain and his settlers built a fortified trading post called a *habitation*, which had three buildings surrounded by a moat and protective wall. He named his settlement Québec after the Algonquian word *kebec*, which means "where the river gets narrow."

Further Exploration

Québec proved to be a good location for the settlement. There was fertile soil nearby, so farms could produce food for

■ Champlain was instrumental in creating the Company of One Hundred Associates. The company was given a monopoly on the fur trade in New France and was concerned not only with trading, but also with converting the Aboriginal population to the Catholic religion.

FURTHER UNDERSTANDING

Fur trade Beaver pelts were in high demand in late sixteenth-century Europe. No other fabric could match the furs in terms of warmth and beauty. Most in demand was the soft underfur of the pelt, which could be made into a felt material far better than any woven fabric. This soft material was made into clothes and wide-brimmed hats. Pelts once worn by Aboriginal peoples were especially in demand because wearing the fur wore off the long guard hairs that protected the soft fur underneath. Fresh pelts were combed in Europe to remove these long guard hairs. Beaver furs were an excellent trade product because they were unavailable in Europe, where the beaver was almost extinct. In addition, the pelts were easily transported, even over long distances.

Northwest Passage Early explorers had hoped that they would find a faster trade route to Asia by sailing west across the Atlantic Ocean. England and France sent explorers to find a route across or around North America. Even though the route was not found until 1845, many areas, such as the St. Lawrence River, Baffin Bay, Davis Strait, and Frobisher Bay, were explored as a result of their efforts.

Stadacona Jacques Cartier had been the first European to visit Stadacona, an Aboriginal settlement, in 1535. By the time of Champlain's visit, the Aboriginal settlement had long disappeared. Champlain's choice of the site for his trading post was not popular with his settlers because some had heard of the difficult winter Cartier had spent there many years before. This is the site of present-day Québec City.

the traders. It was also close to a rich supply of furs and rivers that could be used for transportation. Champlain made friends with the Algonquin and Montagnais peoples who lived nearby so that they would bring their furs to the trading post at Québec. Champlain believed he might find the Northwest Passage in the area. On one trip, he travelled with a group of Aboriginal peoples along the Richelieu River until they reached a large lake. Today, it is called Lake Champlain.

Champlain was interested in exploring further west. At first, his Algonquin allies would not let him. They preferred to control the French trade with the Huron nation to the west. They did not want the French and Huron trading with each other directly.

Finally, after he had proven his loyalty to the Algonquins by supporting them in wars against their enemies, they gave permission for Champlain's exploration west. In 1615, Champlain reached Lake Huron, where he spent time with the Huron people. From there he headed southeast and reached Lake Ontario. He was disappointed because neither of these lakes was the Pacific Ocean. Although unsuccessful in finding the Northwest Passage, Champlain's trip helped solidify French relations with the Huron. They were now firm trade allies.

■ This portrait is believed to be of Champlain. However, there is no authentic portrait of him, and little is known about his background or youth.

The Fur Trade WARS

The French ignored Aboriginal claims to the lands near Québec and began almost immediately to give land to European settlers. Despite this, the local Aboriginal peoples welcomed the French. They viewed the Europeans and their weapons as potential allies against the Iroquois. The Huron and their allies had long been involved in traditional wars of honour against the Iroquois. Once Aboriginal demand for European trade goods was established, wars of economics took over. The Huron and Iroquois competed to control the fur trade with the Europeans.

In 1609, Champlain's Aboriginal allies asked him to fight with them against the Iroquois. Because he depended on his allies for furs, Champlain agreed. He and his men joined a group of Algonquins, Montagnais, and Huron to attack the Iroquois near Lake Champlain. The French guns terrified the Iroquois, who quickly lost the battle. By joining several more battles, Champlain convinced the Huron of his support. By the 1620s, the French received up to two-thirds of their furs from the Huron. The Algonquins now allowed the Huron and French to trade directly because they needed allies against the Iroquois. They also needed agricultural goods from the Huron.

Hostilities between the Huron–French partnership and the Iroquois had by now become a full-fledged war. The Iroquois were trading partners with the English, who were settled along the Hudson River. The English encouraged Iroquois hostility toward the French, hoping to wipe out their fur-trade rivals. As the fur trade grew, the Iroquois wanted to trade more furs with their English partners, but there were no longer many furs on Iroquois lands. They wanted to trade for furs with the Aboriginal groups who lived farther west,

■ Huron warriors often wore wooden armour to protect them in battle. Huron villages were also well fortified against attacks from neighbouring nations, such as the Iroquois.

FURTHER UNDERSTANDING

Hélène Boullé Hélène Boullé was the daughter of a wealthy family, and when Champlain married her, he received 6,000 **livres** from her parents. Her wealth helped fund his expeditions.

Iroquois By the early 1600s, five groups of Iroquois formed the Iroquois Confederacy, also known as the League of Five Nations. This alliance included the Mohawk, Oneida, Onondaga, Cayuga, and Seneca. They hoped to promote peace and order amongst themselves. Representatives of each nation met to solve conflicts between groups and to make decisions. The Confederacy also helped organize the nations during disputes with their enemies. When the Tuscarora joined in the 1700s, the alliance became known as the Six Nations.

but the Huron controlled the water routes to the west.

Iroquois attacks in New France continued into the 1650s, almost defeating the colony. Despite a 1653 peace treaty, the conflict continued in 1658. By this time, the population of New France had grown and was better able to defend itself.

The Fall of Huronia

About 30,000 Huron occupied Huronia, the area to the northeast of Lake Huron. As a result of contact with Europeans, the population of Huronia was exposed to European diseases. This weakened their population greatly, reducing their numbers by about one half.

By 1639, the Iroquois had guns from the English and Dutch traders on the Hudson River. The Dutch guns were better than the French guns sold to the Huron. The Iroquois quickly gained an advantage because they now had far better firepower. Estimates suggest that in 1648, the Huron had about 120 guns, while the Iroquois had more than 500. Part of this unbalance was because the French had a policy of only

selling guns to those Huron who converted to Christianity. Iroquois attacks in the 1640s devastated the Huron. By 1650, the once-powerful Huron nation was destroyed. Many Huron had been killed or had fled their communities to live with other Aboriginal groups.

Challenges Continue

Champlain's wife, Hélène Boullé, joined him in Québec in 1620. They faced many challenges as Champlain devoted himself to his small colony on the St. Lawrence. He worked to establish successful trading alliances and faced conflicts in the fur trade wars. As governor, it was his job to direct the fur trade, defend the colony, act as a judge, make laws, and fight wars. Champlain sent explorers into the interior, tried to attract settlers, and brought missionaries and nuns to convert the Aboriginal peoples to Christianity.

■ After the French joined forces with the Huron in 1615, New France existed under a state of almost constant siege by Iroquois warriors.

■ Hélène Boullé often taught Huron children in the settlement of Québec. After Champlain's death, Hélène became an Ursuline nun in New France.

The Black ROBES

Missionaries felt they had a special duty to teach their Christian beliefs to the Aboriginal peoples.

Although Champlain had trouble attracting settlers to New France while the fur-trade wars were going on, one group of Europeans rushed to North America. These Europeans felt they had a special duty to teach their Christian beliefs to the Aboriginal peoples. They were the missionaries.

Several religious orders sent missionaries to Canada. One of the earliest was the Récollets. Another was the Jesuits. More Jesuits came to Canada than members of any other order.

The early missionaries were from France. They built **mission** settlements among the Aboriginal peoples of eastern Canada. The missions were built in Acadia, along the St. Lawrence River, and among the Huron people near the Great Lakes.

Missionaries in Acadia

The first French missionary who came to Canada was a Roman Catholic named Father Abbé Jessé Fléché. In 1610, he came to the French settlement at Port-Royal with the early fur traders. He stayed at Port-Royal for a year. While he was there, he **baptized** a Mi'kmaq chief named Membertou and twenty members of the chief's family. Fléché returned to France in 1611.

■ Unlike the Récollets, who forced the Huron to become more European in dress, language, and lifestyle, the Jesuits tried to adapt to the Aborginal way of life.

FURTHER UNDERSTANDING

Acadia Acadia was a French colony in the region known today as the Maritimes. The origin of the word *Acadia* is unclear. It may have come from the Aboriginal word *quoddy* or *cadie*, which means "a piece of land," or from the Latin word *archadia*, which means "lands of rural peace." Historians attribute the naming of the area to explorer Giovanni de Verrazzano, who named the region Archadia in reference to its beautiful trees. In ancient Greece, Arcadia referred to an earthly paradise. By the 1620s, the name referred to the whole maritime region.

Black Robes Aboriginal peoples called the Jesuits "black robes," probably because the typical attire of these Catholic priests was long, black robes.

Jesuits Jesuits are a religious order of the Roman Catholic Church. Jesuit missionaries first came to Canada in 1611.

Even though Aboriginal peoples had their own spiritual beliefs, the Jesuits believed it was their duty to convert Aboriginal peoples to the Roman Catholic faith. Many missionaries lived amongst the Aboriginal peoples and learned their languages. They wrote reports about the Aboriginal peoples' ways of life. They also established schools, churches, and hospitals throughout the colony.

Portage A portage is the carrying of boats, canoes, supplies, and goods over land. This might be done to avoid dangerous stretches of water, such as rapids. A portage is also required to travel between two bodies of water which are not connected. Aboriginal groups might travel as far across a lake as possible. They would then carry their canoes to the next river or lake, so their journey could continue.

Two Jesuit priests arrived at Port-Royal in 1611—Father Pierre Biard and Father Enemond Masse. They learned the Mi'kmaq language to help them convert the people to Christianity. The two missionaries taught the Mi'kmaq people Christian prayers and beliefs and baptized some of the adults and children.

In 1676, a Récollet missionary named Father Chrétien Le Clercq came to the Gaspé area. He was the first European to notice that the Mi'kmaq had a kind of writing. He wrote in a report that the Mi'kmaq language was "very beautiful and very rich." The Mi'kmaq people used small drawings called pictographs to show things and ideas. Le Clercq helped the Mi'kmaq invent more pictographs so that they could write down the Christian ideas he discussed.

FATHER JEAN DE BRÉBEUF

Father Jean de Brébeuf was the founder of the Jesuit mission in Huronia. In June 1625, he arrived at Québec and spent his first winter travelling with a group of Montagnais people. In 1626, Brébeuf set off for Huronia. The trip was almost 1,300 kilometres from Québec. Travelling by canoe, it was a long, hard trip, with many portages and mosquitoes. It took almost a month to get there.

Brébeuf lived with the Huron for the next three years, studying their language and way of life. His reports show his love and respect for the Huron people.

In 1629, the English captured Québec and sent all the Jesuit missionaries back to France. Brébeuf returned to Canada in 1633 to build a new mission for the Huron people called Saint-Joseph. Later he built two more settlements.

During the years that Brébeuf lived in Huronia, he wrote a dictionary of the Huron words he learned and translated Christian prayers into the Huron language.

During the 1630s, many of the Huron died of diseases such as **smallpox** and measles, brought by the newcomers from Europe. The Jesuits believed that if people died before they were baptized, their souls would be lost forever. To save souls, they baptized many sick people just before they died. The Huron saw that many of their people died soon after they were baptized. They blamed the black robes for the deaths of their people. They began to threaten the

priests, who had to leave Huronia for a time.

In 1644, Brébeuf returned to live with the Huron. Brébeuf and several other Jesuits were killed in 1649 during an Iroquois attack on their village.

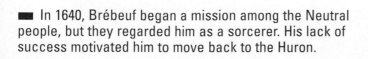

■ In 1640, Brébeuf began a mission among the Neutral people, but they regarded him as a sorcerer. His lack of success motivated him to move back to the Huron.

Father Le Jeune's PLANS

Le Jeune set aside land for Aboriginal peoples who became Christians.

In 1632, Father Paul Le Jeune arrived at Québec. He led the Jesuits in Canada until 1639. During his first winter in Canada, he went with the Montagnais on their winter hunt so that he could learn their language. When he returned to Québec, he formed plans for how the Jesuits could help the Aboriginal peoples living along the St. Lawrence River.

Le Jeune's first plan was to teach the Aboriginal children how to become Christians. His first pupils were a child from a French family and an Aboriginal boy. In 1635, the Jesuits started a school for boys in Québec. By 1636, there were twenty students in the school.

In 1637, Le Jeune tried to make his second plan work. He began to gather the Aboriginal hunters so that he could teach them to be farmers. A rich Frenchman named Noel de Sillery read about Le Jeune's plan and gave him some land near Québec. This land was set aside for Aboriginal peoples who became Christians. It was the first Aboriginal reserve in Canada. However, only a few Aboriginal families came to live in the houses at Sillery.

Le Jeune's plan to care for the sick was more successful. In 1639, a group of French Ursuline nuns arrived at Québec. They helped found the first hospital in Québec.

To raise money for the missionaries and to let other people in the Jesuit order learn about what he was doing, Le Jeune wrote reports about the people and events in Canada. He asked other missionaries to write about their experiences. These reports, called the *Jesuit Relations*, were sent to France each year. The *Jesuit Relations* inspired many French people to give money and land for the missions. Much of what is known about the Aboriginal peoples and the Europeans who lived in early Canada comes from the *Jesuit Relations*.

FURTHER UNDERSTANDING

Jesuit Relations Descriptions of New France written by Jesuit missionaries were translated into several languages. Many Europeans were fascinated by the Jesuits' impressions of life in New France. In one report, Father Le Jeune quoted a Montagnais, who reportedly said, "The beaver does everything well. He provides us with stoves, axes, swords, knives: in fact, the beaver does everything."

When commenting on life among the Huron, another Jesuit wrote, "These people have neither towers, nor cities, nor temples, nor masters of any science or art. They know neither reading nor writing."

Ursuline nuns Ursuline nuns are members of a religious order of the Roman Catholic Church. These women, including Sister Marie de l'Incarnation, established the first school in New France. Aboriginal peoples were urged by the Jesuits to send their daughters to the Ursulines' school. Some girls were interested in the nuns and their lessons. Others resisted, favouring their own beliefs and ways of life.

■ Father Le Jeune's early efforts to preach to the Algonquin were met with laughter, because the man who had taught him the language had, as a joke, taught him a number of foul words instead.

MARIE DE l'INCARNATION

Some of the religious people who came to New France were women. Sister Marie de l'Incarnation was the first leader of the Ursuline nuns in Canada. In May 1639, Sister Marie and a group of nuns sailed to Canada. They came to the settlement at Québec to teach young French and Aboriginal girls. Their first home and school was a rough, two-room shelter. Wind and rain blew through cracks in the walls and the roof, making it hard to keep candles lit.

The little school taught general knowledge, sewing, music, and manners. When it became crowded, the nuns moved to a new building. The new school also had drawbacks. Sister Marie wrote, "The beds are in wood closets and close like cupboards, and although they are lined with cloth, one can hardly get warm."

Sister Marie was a calm, determined person who took disaster in stride. The first winter she was there, smallpox swept through the settlement. Another year, the convent burned down in the middle of winter, and Sister Marie had to find a new home for herself, the nuns, and her students.

Sister Marie looked after the business of the convent and taught her students. After learning several Aboriginal languages, she wrote what she had learned into dictionaries. Sister Marie de l'Incarnation died when she was 73. The convent she founded over 300 years ago still stands in Québec City today.

■ Sister Marie de l'Incarnation was inspired to move to New France after reading Father Le Jeune's *Jesuit Relations*.

■ After the missionaries arrived in New France, they often travelled great distances before they reached an Aboriginal village. Once they reached the village, they began work on the construction of a mission.

Ville-Marie: A Mission in QUÉBEC

France sent soldiers to help defend the settlement at Ville-Marie.

The *Jesuit Relations* aroused great interest among wealthy people in France. In 1640, some of them formed a Roman Catholic missionary society. The society intended to teach Christian beliefs to the Aboriginal peoples in Canada. The society also wanted to provide schools and hospitals. Paul de Chomedey, Sieur de Maisonneuve, was chosen to build a new mission settlement up the river from Québec.

Maisonneuve set sail from France in 1641. With him sailed a group of fifty people who wanted to help start the new mission on the island of Montréal. When the settlers reached Québec, the people advised them not to go any farther. The spot where they planned to build the new settlement lay along an Iroquois trading route. It would be in danger of attack by the Iroquois. After spending the winter in Québec, Maisonneuve insisted that they go on. In the spring of 1642, they reached the mission site and built a fort. This is the site of present-day Montréal.

The fort had a high wall surrounded by a moat and had a cannon at each corner. Inside, the religious settlers built houses and a chapel, and planted peas and corn. They began to meet the Algonquin people who lived nearby. In August, twelve more settlers came to live at the mission. On August 15, the new community held a celebration and named the settlement Ville-Marie.

As the settlers in Québec had warned, Ville-Marie was soon attacked by the Iroquois. One of the members of Maisonneuve's group, Jeanne Mance, was a nurse who hoped to found a hospital for the Aboriginal peoples. Mance gave Maisonneuve money meant for her hospital to hire soldiers to defend the mission.

For several years, the Iroquois tried to make the settlers move away from Ville-Marie. Sometimes the settlers almost gave up, but France sent soldiers to help defend the mission. The settlement at Ville-Marie began to grow. Soon the religious settlers were joined by fur traders and other settlers.

FURTHER UNDERSTANDING

Jeanne Mance At the age of 34, Jeanne Mance volunteered to accompany Maisonneuve to New France. She raised money in France for Hôtel-Dieu, the first hospital in Ville-Marie. This four-room hospital was built outside the fort. Jeanne Mance spent thirty years nursing sick and wounded French and Aboriginal people.

■ The people she cared for called Jeanne Mance the "Angel of the Colony." Under her guidance, the colony grew to 500 people within twenty years.

MARGUERITE BOURGEOYS

In 1652, Marguerite Bourgeoys met Paul de Chomedey, Sieur de Maisonneuve, while he was visiting France. Bourgeoys was a nun in a French convent. She asked Maisonneuve if she could accompany him to Ville-Marie to start a school and a religious community. Maisonneuve agreed.

Bourgeoys landed at Québec in 1653. When she arrived at Ville-Marie, she found there were no school-aged children. She worked hard for the next five years, ironing and washing for the sick and the poor. She also shared her food. Finally she was able to open a school in a stable. There she taught reading, writing, and crafts.

As the school grew, more help was needed. Bourgeoys founded a religious community of teaching sisters. Her teachers did not wait inside the school for students to come to them. Instead, they travelled by canoe or on horseback to teach Aboriginal and French children in their homes along the St. Lawrence River.

In 1676, Bourgeoys opened a boarding school for girls in Ville-Marie. Young women who came from France to marry settlers stayed at the school in Ville-Marie. Men visited the school to meet the Frenchwomen and choose wives. At the school, the women learned the skills they would need to keep house in the settlements after they got married. Bourgeoys also began a mission school in the Aboriginal village of La Montagne.

Bourgeoys spent her last years in Ville-Marie, which by that time was called Montréal. Before her death in January 1700, the people of Montréal had come to believe she was a saint.

■ The Sisters of the Congregation of Notre-Dame, founded by Marguerite Bourgeoys, now number several thousand.

■ Montréal was originally founded as a Catholic mission called Ville-Marie.

Slow Progress in NEW FRANCE

As late as 1643, Québec relied on Aboriginal peoples for its supply of food.

Despite the efforts of Champlain, the Jesuits, the nuns, and other settlers, New France grew slowly. In 1627, there were fewer than 100 European settlers in New France. Only fifteen Aboriginal people had converted to the Christian faith.

The colony's economy was precarious. During the wars with the Iroquois, the fur trade almost came to a stop. Few people in France were willing to come to New France. They heard of the frightening Iroquois raids and the difficult Canadian winters. Even offers of land and greater social freedoms were not enough to entice many settlers.

In addition, the economy of New France did not require many Europeans. Most of the work in the fur trade was done by Aboriginal peoples. As late as 1643, Québec relied on Aboriginal peoples for its supply of food. Farming was not successful because, with the exception of the small settlement, there was no market for agricultural products. The Huron would not allow the French to compete for agricultural markets. After the destruction of Huronia, however, French farms near Québec increased their trade with the Algonquins. This helped increase the colony's attractiveness to settlers.

The Company of One Hundred Associates

The king of France, Louis XIII, was unhappy with the slow growth of New France. He gave control of the colony to the Company of One Hundred Associates in 1627. This French company promised to settle 4,000 Roman Catholics along the St. Lawrence within fifteen years. In exchange,

■ The Jesuit mission in Huronia, Sainte-Marie, was home to some sixty French people. It consisted of a chapel, storehouses, and sleeping quarters. The mission was destroyed in 1649 to prevent it from falling into the hands of the Iroquois.

FURTHER UNDERSTANDING

Treaty A treaty is a signed agreement between two or more countries. Wars in Europe affected the colonies of North America. In their efforts to resolve conflicts, England and France negotiated for territory. With various treaties, they transferred control of different areas in North America between them.

they were granted control of the fur trade from Florida to the Arctic Circle and from Newfoundland to the Great Lakes and beyond. The French king hoped that this private company would create a successful colony in New France. The results were bitterly disappointing.

In 1628, the Company's first large shipment of settlers and supplies was sent to Québec. It was captured by English ships, which nearly ruined the Company. When war between England and France broke out the following year, an English raiding party surrounded Québec and prevented supplies from reaching the settlement. After a hard winter, with the settlers facing starvation, Champlain surrendered the colony. Most of the settlers returned to France. Three years later, when the colony was restored to France by a peace treaty, Champlain found that most of the buildings at Québec had been burned to the ground. The Company of One Hundred Associates continued its work in New France, but never fully recovered from its losses.

The Colony Falters

The colony had many difficulties to overcome. Continued Iroquois hostility reduced the Company's profits and discouraged people from coming to North America. The settlers often argued among themselves. The governor appointed by the Company argued with the **clergy**, and the clergy quarrelled with the merchants and the fur traders. The most serious dispute was about trading liquor to Aboriginal peoples for beaver pelts. The clergy wanted the governor to stop this practice, but the fur traders said it would reduce their profits. Soon the bishop and the governor clashed over the issue.

New France was barely surviving when Champlain died on Christmas Day, 1635. He was buried with much ceremony, and a chapel was built over his grave. Because the chapel later burned down, the burial site of the "Father of New France" is unknown. It is thought to be somewhere under present-day Québec City.

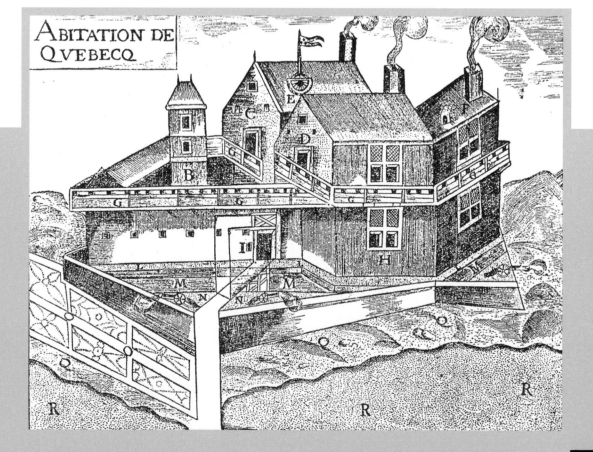

■ Champlain founded Québec in 1608. The first habitation consisted of three lodgings protected by a ditch and palisades. Among those living at the habitation were workers and craftspeople. The habitation stored arms and provisions.

King Louis XIV Takes ACTION

In 1665, Louis XIV sent 1,200 battle-hardened soldiers to the colony.

By 1660, the French colony on the St. Lawrence was in a desperate situation. Settlement under company rule had only increased the population to about 2,000. More than half of these people were born in North America. Less than one percent of the granted land was being used. New France was in constant danger from the Iroquois and the British. The economy depended on the fur trade, and the people were still not self-sufficient in terms of food production.

Louis XIV wanted New France to become the centre of a mighty empire. When New France pleaded for help, Louis took action. King Louis XIV was determined to save New France. He cancelled the **charter** of the Company of One Hundred Associates in 1663, and selected his own officials to run the colony.

In 1665, he sent 1,200 battle-hardened soldiers to the colony. The regiment's first expedition into Iroquois territory set out in mid-winter. Unused to wearing snowshoes, finding their own food, and living in cold temperatures, the soldiers were lucky to return alive. The next fall, a larger force invaded Iroquois land. It met very few Iroquois, who avoided direct conflict with the well-armed French soldiers. Before returning to New France, the soldiers raided temporarily deserted Iroquois villages, burned the crops, and destroyed the people's stores of food.

The Mohawk people, the largest and most powerful of the Iroquois nations, were badly shaken by the raid. Further weakened by smallpox, the Iroquois made peace in 1667. However, conflict did not end until 1690.

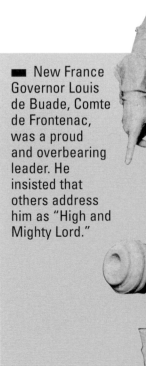

■ New France Governor Louis de Buade, Comte de Frontenac, was a proud and overbearing leader. He insisted that others address him as "High and Mighty Lord."

FURTHER UNDERSTANDING

Bishop François de Laval, a Jesuit priest, was appointed the first bishop in New France in 1674. One of his major accomplishments was founding a seminary in New France, where priests could be trained. This later became known as Laval University.

Empire England and France were in continuous competition for control of areas around the world. Their ambitious plans included the colonies in North America. By gaining control over other countries or states, France and England each hoped to expand their own empire, thereby increasing their wealth and power.

Intendant Jean Talon became the first intendant of New France in 1665. He wanted to expand the economy by developing industries, such as mining and lumber. He also started a brewery and had a shipyard built.

King Louis XIV The seventy-two-year reign of King Louis XIV was the longest in European history. Upon the death of his father, King Louis XIII, he became the king of France at the age of 4. The country flourished under Louis XIV's leadership. His patronage of the arts and successful military campaigns made France the envy of other nations.

GOVERNING NEW FRANCE

Louis XIV made New France a French province and gave it an administration like other French provinces. The most important official in New France was the governor. As the king's personal representative, he headed all ceremonies and meetings. Because he was **commander-in-chief** of the armed forces, he was usually a professional soldier.

The second-most important official was the intendant. He managed the daily affairs of the colony, including the colony's economy. He kept order and passed laws for the general well-being of the community.

The bishop was the third-most important official in New France. Though he was appointed by the Pope in Rome, the king of France had to find him acceptable. Both the bishop and the Catholic missionaries needed the king's help to carry out their work in New France.

New France was divided into sections, or districts. Each district provided men to defend the colony. The intendant chose a respected settler to be the captain of the militia in each district. This person acted as a link between the people and the government. He informed the people of the intendant's plans, and reported the people's concerns to the intendant.

Each year, officials in New France wrote long reports of what had happened during the year and sent them to France before the St. Lawrence River froze. In France, the king's minister in charge of the colonies received these reports. He decided which problems to discuss with the king and, the following spring, sent the king's instructions back to New France.

■ Louis XIV's royal emblem was the Sun. He is known as the "Sun King."

Talon Helps New France GROW

Talon promised free land and eighteen months full pay to any soldier who would stay in the colony.

Louis XIV made Jean-Baptiste Colbert his minister in charge of the colonies. Colbert viewed the colonies as a source of **raw materials** for France. French firms would turn these raw materials into manufactured goods. The goods would then be sold back to colonies such as New France. For this plan to succeed, the population of New France would have to be greatly increased so that a market would exist for the manufactured goods.

Colbert's most important task was to choose the colony's first intendant. It was difficult to find a talented person who was also willing to travel to New France. In 1665, Colbert found the man he wanted, and Jean Talon was appointed to the post.

Talon wanted to make New France attractive to settlers. He promised free land and eighteen months full pay to any soldier who would stay in the colony. This was more money than the soldiers had ever had at one time. More than four hundred officers and soldiers who had been sent to defend the colony from the Iroquois decided to remain. Talon also reduced the cost of the ocean voyage to New France, and promised higher wages to skilled craftspeople who settled in the colony.

Since there were few French women in New France, Talon asked the king to send unmarried women to be wives of the soldiers and settlers. Nearly eight hundred women and girls came between 1663 and 1673. Among those recruited were orphans raised at the government's expense. These women were called *les filles du roi*, meaning "daughters of the king." When they married, Louis XIV provided each a dowry of one ox, one cow, two pigs, two chickens, two barrels of salt beef, and money.

The success of these policies can be judged by looking at census figures. From 1665 to 1680, about 6,000 people came to the colony. After this time, the population of New France continued to grow because of high birth rates.

FURTHER UNDERSTANDING

Census Information gathered to find out the official count of people living in an area may be organized by categories, such as age groups, occupations, or origin. Jean Talon conducted a census of the population of New France. Although various plans to increase the population were underway, he feared that many people were also leaving the colony. Tracking this information would allow officials to see if their goal of populating the colony was being met.

Dowry Many of *les filles du roi* were orphans in France. Many were very poor, and the king provided their dowry. A dowry is the property and other valuables that a bride brings to her husband when they are married. As a result of their dowries, *les filles du roi* had better prospects and many marriage choices in New France.

■ Although he was the French minister in charge of the colonies, Jean-Baptiste Colbert never visited New France.

NEW FAMILIES

One way of increasing population is to encourage large families. A 1670 law stated that all inhabitants of New France who had up to ten living children would be paid 300 livres yearly, and those who had twelve children, 400 livres. In addition, the law stated "it is the king's will that all males who marry before the age of 16 will receive on their wedding day 20 livres to be known as the king's gift." The king also tried to encourage marriage by forbidding bachelors from trading with the Aboriginal peoples, and by making fathers with unmarried sons over 19 years of age, or unmarried daughters over 15 years, pay a fine.

The European Population of New France

Year	Population
1608	28
1628	76
1641	240
1663	2,500
1665	3,220
1668	6,280
1679	9,840
1685	10,730
1695	12,790
1706	16,420
1719	22,530
1734	37,100
1739	42,700
1754	55,000

■ In 1665, Jean Talon was sent by King Louis XIV to monitor the population of New France. During his stay, the population increased by more than 4,000 people.

The Fur Trade Heads **WEST**

Between 1689 and 1713, New France was almost constantly at war with British traders.

While New France struggled to grow, another struggle was taking place in the north. It was the struggle to control the fur trade. In 1670, the British government granted all the territory surrounding the rivers that flowed into Hudson Bay to the Hudson's Bay Company for the fur trade. This area, about 4 million square kilometres, was named Rupert's Land.

To better compete with the Hudson's Bay Company, French adventurers explored to the west and south of the Great Lakes. Louis Jolliet and Father Jacques Marquette found the Mississippi River in 1673. Nine years later, thinking that this river led to China, Robert de la Salle followed the Mississippi to the Gulf of Mexico. He claimed all the land drained by the river for France and named it Louisiana.

Everywhere the French traders and explorers went, they established forts and trading posts on the best waterways. These forts were necessary, for between 1689 and 1713, New France was almost constantly at war with the British traders to the south and the Hudson's Bay Company to the north. New France feared it was losing hold of the fur trade.

■ Throughout his career, explorer Robert de la Salle hoped to discover the sea passage to China. La Salle named the land above Montréal that he claimed for France "La Chine." Today, it is known as Lachine.

FURTHER UNDERSTANDING

Robert de la Salle La Salle was an ambitious French explorer and a successful fur trader. He established several colonies and trading posts, including one at Fort Frontenac, near present-day Kingston, Ontario. La Salle claimed territory for France that stretched from the Appalachian Mountains in the east, all the way to the Rocky Mountains in the west, and from the Great Lakes south to the Gulf of Mexico. He was an aggressive leader. During his last expedition in 1687, some of his men rebelled against him and he was murdered.

RADISSON AND DES GROSEILLIERS

Pierre-Esprit Radisson and his brother-in-law, Médard Chouart Des Groseilliers, were French fur traders from Trois-Rivières. They explored the area north of the Great Lakes looking for furs. The Aboriginal peoples they met told them there were plenty of beavers farther north, toward Hudson Bay.

The partners travelled north and returned from their explorations with sixty canoes filled with furs. They expected a warm welcome. However, the officials at Québec thought too many young men were leaving the settlement to live and trade with the Aboriginal peoples. They had decided that no one could trade furs without a licence. Since Radisson and Des Groseilliers did not have trading licences, they were fined and their furs were taken away.

The two traders were furious, so they sailed to England, where the king agreed to let them trade for furs around Hudson Bay. In June 1668, they set off for North America in two ships. Storms forced Radisson's ship to return to England, but Des Groseilliers' ship, the *Nonsuch*, continued on. That year, Des Groseilliers built a small trading post on Hudson Bay. In the spring, he and his crew traded with a large group of Aboriginal people. When Des Groseilliers' ship returned to England, it carried a large cargo of furs.

Des Groseilliers' journey proved to the English that they could avoid the French stronghold on the St. Lawrence to reach the rich furs of the west. The English merchants were delighted. In 1670, they started the Hudson's Bay Company.

As the French and English laid claim to various fur-trading areas, they did not ask permission of the Aboriginal peoples who lived there.

Radisson established the company's Nelson River fort and stayed there as its guide and translator. There were now two important fur-trading areas in North America. The English traded on Hudson Bay. The French traded along the St. Lawrence River and the Great Lakes.

Due to a disagreement with the company, Radisson and Des Groseilliers abandoned English interest for French interest in 1674. Jean-Baptiste Colbert had made them a generous offer they could not refuse. The brothers-in-law worked for the French in the Hudson Bay area for many years, helping undermine the Hudson's Bay Company's hold. In 1684, the two opportunists were once again in trouble with France. Radisson defected back to the English and became the chief trader at Fort Nelson from 1685 to 1687. He eventually retired in England. Des Groseilliers returned to New France and retired there.

■ The early French fur traders who left the colony of New France to collect furs and live among the Native Peoples were known as the *coureurs de bois*. This French term means "runners of the woods." The coureurs de bois travelled the St. Lawrence River in canoes trading furs, often illegally. These traders were later given licences and became know as the *voyageurs*.

The Hudson's Bay COMPANY

The English and the French had different ways of trading.

The English who worked for the Hudson's Bay Company built trading posts on the shores of Hudson Bay. They were called factories because the person in charge was called a chief factor. The factories were built where rivers flowed into the bay, so it was easy for Aboriginal peoples to bring their furs to the posts.

Many people worked at the company factories. The chief factor, the clerk, and sometimes a junior clerk did the trading. Other people, such as doctors, carpenters, and tailors, also lived at the posts. However, the English fur traders did not try to build lasting settlements as the French did. The English who came to Hudson Bay were interested only in trading for furs, not in establishing a colony.

The English and the French had different ways of trading. Instead of travelling to trade with the Aboriginal peoples, which is what the French did, the English company traders stayed at their trading posts and waited for the Aboriginal peoples to bring their furs to them.

■ The York Factory was built in 1788 near Hudson Bay. As this location was accessible to ocean-going vessels, the valuable goods manufactured at the post could easily be transported to Europe.

HENRY KELSEY

Henry Kelsey joined the Hudson's Bay Company as a clerk when he was only 17 years old. He went to York Factory, near present-day Churchill, Manitoba, to work at the trading post. Kelsey worked for the company for forty years. The Cree who came to trade their furs at York Factory became Kelsey's friends. He learned to speak their language and made several trips with them along the coast of Hudson Bay.

In 1690, the Hudson's Bay Company sent Kelsey south on a trip. He was sent to invite the Assiniboine to trade at Hudson Bay. He travelled with a group of Cree returning to their homeland in the southwest. On the long journey by canoe, the men and women in the group shared the work.

When Kelsey reached the prairie grasslands, he left his Cree guides and went farther west on foot to find the Assiniboine. He met the Assiniboine and spent two years hunting with them before returning home to York Factory. Kelsey had opened up a new trading area for the Hudson's Bay Company and had been the first European to travel that far west. His accounts of his journey include descriptions of bison, grizzly bears, and Aboriginal groups that are believed to have been the Sioux or Gros Ventre.

■ In the fall of 1690, when Henry Kelsey reached the prairies, he had travelled farther west than any other European explorer. It would be another 100 years before the next European would travel as far west.

Pierre de La VÉRENDRYE

The French wanted to trade for furs farther west because there were not many furs left in the Great Lakes area.

The French wanted to trade for furs farther west because there were not many furs left in the Great Lakes area. In 1731, a French trader and explorer named Pierre de La Vérendrye set out from a French trading post on Lake Superior. With him were his sons and his nephew. Aboriginal peoples helped the group find their way.

They travelled toward the fur country in the west. It was a difficult route, with many portages. On their journey, the traders built new fur-trading posts for the French. In 1732, La Vérendrye reached Lake of the Woods, where he built a large post. In 1734,

La Vérendrye and his family reached a spot near Lake Winnipeg where they built a trading post called Fort Maurepas. They continued west to explore the Prairies and build new trading posts. They found that the Saskatchewan River was the best route west to lands where furs were plentiful.

La Vérendrye and his family worked hard to trade with the Aboriginal peoples they met. They told the Aboriginal peoples that it was better and easier for them to trade with the French than with the English at their posts on Hudson Bay. They were largely successful, and the French fur trade grew.

■ When Pierre de La Vérendrye died at the age of 62, he was in the process of organizing yet another expedition to the West.

The VOYAGEURS

In the 1750s, the Seven Years' War broke out between France and England. When the war ended, England had won control of the French settlements in North America. Some Scottish fur traders in New York decided to move to Montréal to run the fur trade there. They believed they could make more money.

The Scots used the French trading posts and took over the French fur-trading companies. The Scots hired many expert French traders called *voyageurs* to trade with the Aboriginal peoples. Some of the voyageurs had learned to speak Aboriginal languages and married Aboriginal women. They knew the routes inland to the best fur country. The voyageurs transported the furs back to the merchants.

Some voyageurs travelled thousands of kilometres by canoe to explore and trade where no Europeans had ever been before. By the 1780s, there were many small fur-trading companies in Montréal. They competed with one another, making it difficult for anyone to make a living. Some of the merchants decided to join together to improve their businesses. In 1783, they formed the North West Company. The Nor'Westers, as the traders came to be called, spent the winter collecting furs from the Aboriginal peoples to the west.

The Montréal merchants had problems getting supplies and goods to their trading posts in the west. Canoe travel was expensive and took a long time. To solve this problem, the Nor'Westers built a large trading centre on Lake Superior called Fort William. Each summer, merchants from Montréal took supplies and trading goods to Fort William. There they met their wintering partners, who came with canoes filled with furs from the inland posts.

The North West Company and the Hudson's Bay Company became bitter rivals. After a hundred years of the Aboriginal peoples coming to its trading posts on the bay, the Hudson's Bay Company had to change. It began to build inland trading posts, too. However, the Nor'Westers dominated the western trade. By 1795, the North West Company controlled over two-thirds of the Canadian fur trade.

> The voyageurs knew the routes inland to the best fur country.

FURTHER UNDERSTANDING

Seven Years' War Lasting from 1756 to 1763, the Seven Years' War was the final battle for control of North America. Britain and France continued to fight for control of land, the fur trade, and fishing grounds in North America. This war ended in 1763 when the Treaty of Paris was signed. France surrendered almost all of its land in North America to the British.

Voyageurs These skilled French fur traders, working for fur-trading companies, were licensed to trade with the Aboriginal peoples. Voyageurs paddled and portaged canoes loaded with trade goods and furs. They lived a life of adventure and hard work and often travelled across the country in groups called fur brigades.

Many of the canoes used by the voyageurs were made from birchbark. The canoes were easily damaged by river rapids and the heavy loads the fur traders carried with them.

Mackenzie's QUEST

Mackenzie was the first European to cross North America to the Pacific Ocean.

Alexander Mackenzie led the Nor'Westers' inland expansion. In 1787, Mackenzie became a partner in the North West Company and was sent to the company's post on the Athabasca River. He was second-in-command to Peter Pond, who had explored the region around the Athabascan post. Pond was convinced that the large river flowing west from Great Slave Lake would ultimately lead to the Pacific Ocean. Mackenzie was intrigued.

Mackenzie set out in 1789 to follow the river to its source, but found it went north to the Arctic, not west to the Pacific. This river is now named after him—the Mackenzie River. In 1793, Mackenzie decided to try again, this time following waters heading west from the upper Peace River. This time, he crossed the **Continental Divide** to the Fraser River. After discussing his plan with Aboriginal peoples he met there, Mackenzie took their advice and headed overland instead of continuing on the river. Eventually following the Bella Coola River to its mouth, Mackenzie became the first European to cross North America to the Pacific Ocean.

FURTHER UNDERSTANDING

Pemmican Some Aboriginal groups prepared this food by drying meat over a fire or in the air. It was then pounded into a powder and mixed with melted fat and sometimes berries. This was an effective way to preserve the meat. Pemmican is also lightweight and compact, so it can be easily carried. For these reasons, pemmican was an excellent food for Nor'Westers and voyageurs who travelled west.

Peter Pond A fur trader from Connecticut, Peter Pond helped to extend the fur trade west when he established a small fort on the Athabasca River, near Lake Athabasca. He developed his theory about a route from Great Slave Lake to the Pacific Ocean from stories told by Aboriginal people in the area.

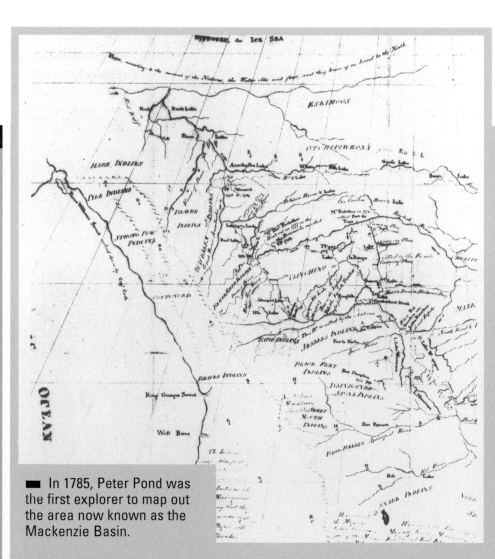

■ In 1785, Peter Pond was the first explorer to map out the area now known as the Mackenzie Basin.

ABORIGINAL WOMEN AND THE FUR TRADE

Aboriginal women played an important role in the fur trade. Without their skills and hard work, the fur trade would not have been possible. Many of the fur traders married Aboriginal women. These women did much of the work at the fur-trading posts.

Aboriginal women often went on fur-trading trips with their husbands. Many acted as guides. They worked with the men to paddle the canoes and carried heavy loads across portages. They set up camp when they stopped, and prepared meals.

Aboriginal women had many skills important to the fur traders. Women made or helped make many items of value. They prepared food such as pemmican. Sometimes Aboriginal women trapped smaller animals for meat and fur. The women were skilled at cleaning and preparing pelts and hides. They made blankets and clothing, including moccasins. They helped make snowshoes. The men made the frames of snowshoes, and the women made the webbing for them. They gathered and split spruce roots used to make birchbark canoes. They also collected spruce gum, which was used to make the canoes waterproof. Aboriginal women also knew how to make medicines from plants.

The fur traders learned many skills from their Aboriginal wives. They learned the languages and customs of their wives' people. If a woman from an Aboriginal group married a trader, she often acted as an interpreter and peacemaker among her people and the traders. This improved trading relationships.

■ The pemmican made by Aboriginal women was stored in folded rawhide containers called "parfleches." These containers were designed to keep out air and moisture. As a result, the pemmican could stay fresh for several years.

In Search of FURS

By the seventeenth century, France and England had marked their claims in North America. As explorers on both sides sought out new territory and furs, competition between the two powers increased. This map shows French and English land claims in North America in the first half of the seventeenth century.

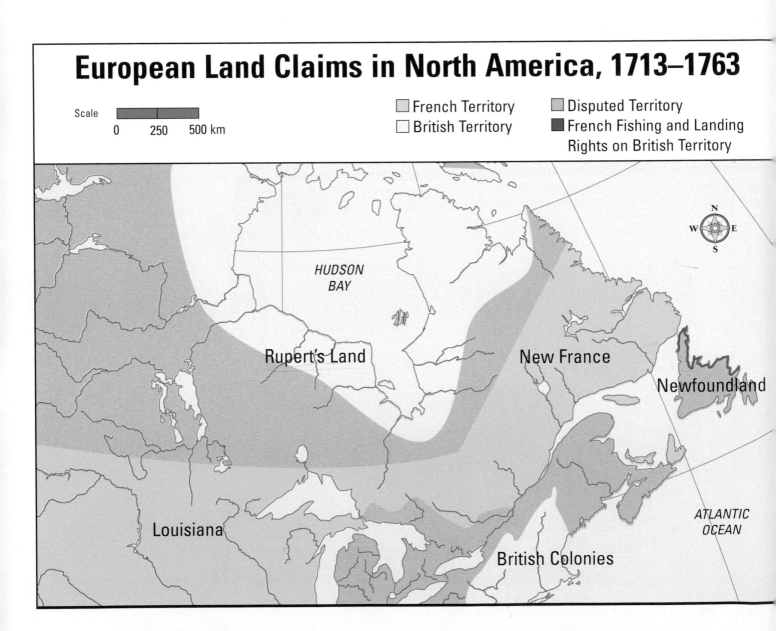

European Land Claims in North America, 1713–1763

Scale

0   250   500 km

☐ French Territory
☐ British Territory
☐ Disputed Territory
■ French Fishing and Landing Rights on British Territory

HUDSON BAY

Rupert's Land

New France

Newfoundland

Louisiana

British Colonies

ATLANTIC OCEAN

N
W E
S

At first, the Europeans only traded with the Aboriginal peoples in the summer. Then they sailed home to Europe for the winter. As the fur trade grew, some traders and merchants decided to stay and live in North America so that they could trade for furs all year round. The furs were collected at the trading posts and were then taken to Europe and sold. This map shows some of the most important trading posts around 1760.

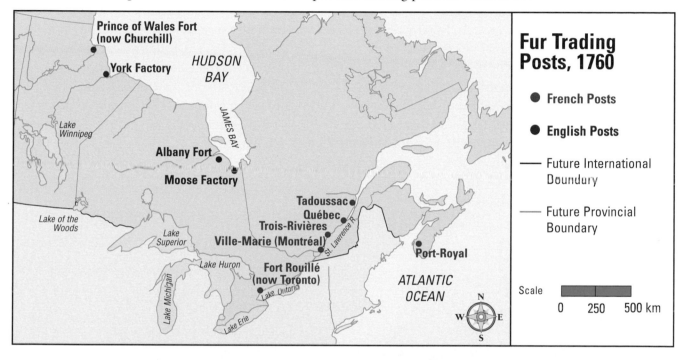

The early European explorers in North America were motivated by a variety of differing goals. Some searched for the fabled Northwest Passage, while others sought to expand the reaches of the fur trade. All succeeded in opening up the great expanse of land that would become Canada. This map illustrates a few of the many voyages west.

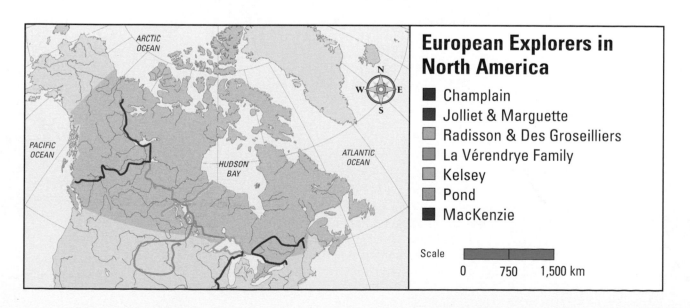

New France THRIVES

By the end of French rule in Canada in 1763, there were about 250 seigneuries and 9,000 farms.

The king of France, Louis XIII, granted much of the land in New France to nobles, religious orders, the Company of One Hundred Associates, and other important people. These landowners were called seigneurs. Some of the largest blocks of land belonged to the Catholic church. In return for the free land, the seigneurs promised to divide it into smaller units for new settlers, who were called *habitants*.

The distribution of land between seigneurs and habitants was called the seigneurial system. By the end of French rule in Canada in 1763, there were about 250 seigneuries and 9,000 farms.

The farm lots were long and narrow so that each farm would have access to water. A farm was usually 30 to 35 hectares and included a wood lot for fuel. Many French Canadians built their homes about 1 kilometre from the river. When all the river frontage was taken, the seigneur opened a second row of farms behind the first row. The settlers cleared the land in front of their houses to make a road parallel to the St. Lawrence River. The houses in a seigneury were spread along a road, instead of being gathered together in a village.

FURTHER UNDERSTANDING

Habitants A habitant was a French-Canadian farmer. Marie and Louis Hébert were the first French farmers to settle in New France. They built their home in Québec in 1617. They were hard-working settlers. They planted corn and other vegetables, and experimented with vines and apples. Hébert's skills as a druggist put him on good terms with Aboriginal peoples. However, he was not allowed to trade with them because the Company of One Hundred Associates had control of the fur trade.

Seigneurs Seigneurs held high status in the community. Once established, a seigneur enjoyed prosperity and privileges. The French system was different from most European countries, which did not allow women to hold land. One of the first women to hold a seigneury was Madeleine d'Allone.

■ Many of the farmers in New France lived on small sections of land called "seigneuries." The king of France granted these plots to the colony's upper class, who rented them to the colony's new settlers.

Rights and Duties of Seigneurs and Habitants

The seigneur's duties included:
- granting land to each settler,
- keeping a manor or house on the land,
- reporting on the crops to the intendant,
- building a flour mill for the habitants,
- creating a court for settling disputes, and
- paying a tax if the land was sold.

The seigneur's privileges included:
- having each habitant help with his crops three or four days a year,
- having the best pew in the church,
- receiving rent and dues from habitants, and
- charging for the use of the mill, the common pasture, and for fishing.

In exchange for the land, the habitants had to:
- live on and cultivate the land,
- pay a small sum of money, called the *cens*, each year to the seigneur,
- pay a larger, fixed sum of money, called the *rente*, each year,
- work a few days a year on the seigneur's land,
- give one-fourteenth of the grain ground in the mill to the seigneur,
- pay a tax if land was sold outside the family,
- give the seigneur one-tenth of all the fish caught each year, and
- pay the seigneur for use of the common land for cutting firewood or grazing animals.

FARMING IN NEW FRANCE

Starting a farm was back-breaking work. Using only simple tools, the farmer had to clear the land of trees and rocks, build a home, and plant crops. It sometimes took several generations before the land was completely cleared.

The habitants produced almost everything they needed, including their own furniture and clothes. Most habitants had a large garden of corn, cabbages, squash, onions, and other vegetables. One visitor to New France commented that many people "can be smelled when they pass by on account of their frequent use of onions." Fruit trees produced cherries, pears, plums, and apples for eating and making into cider. A small tobacco patch supplied tobacco for clay pipes. The forest and meadows provided geese and moose, and the rivers teemed with fish. The habitants picked currants, strawberries, and mulberries. Maple sap was boiled down into syrup.

Meat was preserved in the fall by smoking it or soaking it in salt water. Pork preserved the best. The usual drinks were water, spruce beer, or red wine mixed with water. In times of war or poor harvests, the habitants had to make do with much less food. This happened often in the new colony. Seventeen times between 1700 and 1760, crop failures forced the government to import wheat from France.

■ Louis Hébert, his wife, and their three children were the first French settlers to support themselves by farming.

Life in New FRANCE

The average French Canadian lived much better than did the peasants in France.

Sanitary conditions in the colony were poor. There were no indoor toilets. People used chamber pots and dumped the contents out the window in the morning. Garbage was left on village streets. Few people washed more than once a week, and clothes were worn for months at a time without being washed. As a result of these conditions, settlers in New France suffered many illnesses and epidemics.

Despite hardships, the average French Canadian lived much better than the **peasants** in France. The habitants owned their own homes, grew their own food, and breathed fresh air. They were independent.

The women in New France were known for their wit and sense of humour. The men were observed to be always cheerful and in a good mood. They were deeply courageous and believed that nothing was impossible.

Few habitants travelled on foot. They drove carriages in summer and in winter they used sleighs. In New France, a horse was as important to the habitants as an automobile is to people today. Men rode their best horses to impress their neighbours.

The people in New France copied French fashions. However, since communication with Europe was slow, French-Canadian clothing was usually behind current styles. Visitors from France were often amused by the women who wore skirts much shorter than the fashion in France. In the home, women wore large smocks, and when they left the house, they put on a hooded cloak. Upper-class men and women wore wigs. On Sundays everyone dressed in their best. Upper-class women curled and powdered their hair, put on jewellery, and wore high-heeled shoes.

FURTHER UNDERSTANDING

Epidemics Smallpox, measles, whooping cough, and fevers spread quickly in the colony. In 1702, smallpox killed about 8 percent of the population.

Loyalists People who remain loyal to the ruling government or monarchy are called Loyalists. Colonists in the thirteen British colonies, along what is now the east coast of the United States, were in conflict during the American Revolution (1775–1783). Some colonists were Loyalists, wishing to remain loyal to Britain. Others wished to become independent of Britain. Many Loyalists travelled north to escape the aggression of American rebels.

■ The male habitant typically wore an overcoat tied with a traditional woven sash. On their heads, they wore knitted toques.

SLAVERY

Slavery was common in seventeenth- and eighteenth-century New France. Owning a slave was a sign of importance. The governors had slaves, as did merchants, priests, and women's religious orders. Between 1680 and 1800, there were about 4,000 slaves in the colony. Around a quarter of these were African in origin, brought north by Loyalists after the American Revolution. The rest of the slaves were Aboriginal peoples. The Aboriginal peoples who were allies of the French supplied the colony with people captured from other Aboriginal groups.

Owners often traded their slaves. In 1722, records show that an African woman was sold for a pig and some peas. Slaves could marry only with their owner's permission. Children born of slaves became the owner's property. Owners were required to feed, clothe, and house their slaves, and to care for them when they became old and sick. Young children could not be separated from their parents.

Aboriginal peoples sold into slavery died at an average age of 18. The average African slave lived to be 25 years old. In comparison, the average life span of a French Canadian was 50 years.

Slavery was never suitable for the French-Canadian system of agriculture and business, so it never became as important as it did in the southern United States. Nevertheless, it remained legal until 1834, when legislation made it illegal in the British Empire.

■■ Festive social gatherings were a very important part of life in New France. All members of the colony, both the upper and lower classes, often joined together to dance and celebrate important events.

The CHURCH

The Catholic clergy in New France were very influential, and the church itself was wealthy and powerful.

Religion played a major role in the life of New France. Because France was a Catholic country, almost everyone in the colony was Roman Catholic. Protestants were not allowed to get married in New France or to bring their families to the colony. "Everyone knows," explained Québec's first Bishop, François de Laval, "that Protestants are not as loyal to the king as are the Catholics."

The Catholic clergy in New France was very influential, and the church itself was wealthy and powerful. The priests were among the few educated people in the colony. The church ran the schools and hospitals and looked after the poor, the sick, and the homeless.

Village life centred on the local church. The priest made public announcements from the pulpit, and even music and paintings had religious themes. The priest cared for people from baptism to marriage to death. He advised, comforted, warned, and helped the people of New France. All Catholics were required to give a portion of their income or farm produce, called a *tithe*, each year to support the church.

The church also tried to make sure that the people lived moral lives. It regulated everything from clothing styles to language. One bishop told the governor that since his daughter "needs recreation because of her

age, she may be allowed a few decent and moderate dances, but only with persons of her own sex, and always in the presence of her mother as a safeguard against indecent words and songs; but never with men and boys."

Other bishops warned women against going outside without a proper hat. The church told the people what to read, wear, sing, dance, drink, and think.

While the church tried to influence all aspects of the habitants' lives, it was not always successful. Many people did not always do what the priests wanted them to do. Many habitants continued to wear what they wanted. At times, the government had to force the habitants to pay their tithes, especially during times of drought when crops were ruined.

■ The Notre-Dame-des-Victoires is one of the oldest Catholic churches in Québec. Construction began in 1688 and finished in 1723. The church has been rebuilt and restored several times since.

FURTHER UNDERSTANDING

Protestantism One of the divisions of Christianity, Protestantism was the result of the Reformation, which was a movement in the sixteenth century to reform the Christian church. Protestantism is divided into many movements, one of which began in England and is known as Anglicanism. The Church of England became Protestant in the sixteenth century. The often violent conflicts between Protestants and Catholics helped fuel the rivalry between Protestant England and Catholic France.

MARRIAGE

The law allowed girls to marry when they turned 12. Boys could marry at 14. In the early years of the colony, there were so few women that girls married when they were very young. In 1663, there were six bachelors for every female of child-bearing age. The 800 *filles du roi* whom the king sent to the colony found husbands within a few days. When a woman became a widow, men began to court her almost immediately.

As the colony became more established, couples did not rush into marriage as quickly. The average age of marriage for women increased to 22.5. For men it was 26.5. Other people waited until they were 30 years old before marrying. A woman needed her parents' consent to marry until she was 25, while men needed consent until they were 30.

Most people married within their social class. Parents wanted their children to marry into a family that would benefit them financially. Few people married solely for love. Men wanted strong, healthy, hard-working wives who would provide them with many children. Women desired husbands who could protect and provide for them. Most marriages took place in the winter when there was less work to do on the farm. The bride's family was expected to give the husband a dowry of money, furniture, or agricultural produce.

■ Between the years 1663 and 1673, a number of young women immigrated to New France to marry and bear children for the colony. These women were known as *les filles du roi* because their expenses and dowries were paid for by the king of France.

Children in New FRANCE

Sixteen percent of the families in New France had ten to fourteen children.

New France was a young community. In 1706, almost half the population was under 15 years of age. Children were important to families because they helped with farm work and looked after their parents in their old age. Children were expected to help with chores by age 7. Most families had several children. Sixteen percent of the families in New France had ten to fourteen children. As a result of this high birth rate, the population almost doubled every twenty-five years between 1679 and 1754.

The birth of a child was one of the most important events in the community. The women in the area helped with the birth. Children were born at home, not in one of the few hospitals.

Names from the Bible were most popular. Girls were often named Marie. Boys were often called Joseph. The second name was usually the name of a godparent, although the child was frequently called by its last, or family, name. The baby's behaviour at the christening was important. If it howled and cried, it was said that the child would grow up with a good singing voice. A quiet baby was thought to be a sleepy-head.

The godfather paid the priest to ring the church bells at the christening. If the bells rang for only a short time, the people said the godfather was stingy. The people also thought that the louder the bells rang, the more the sound would clear the baby's ears.

A Child's Education

Most children in New France received some education. However, the government did not require children to go to school, and they often stayed home to help with harvesting or planting.

Schools were run by the church. Pupils learned about Roman Catholicism, proper

■ The people of New France made their own candles using the tallow from the fat of cows, sheep, or pigs. A candle-making machine moulded the tallow into the shape of candles.

FURTHER UNDERSTANDING

Abacus Instead of a calculator, people used an instrument made of a frame with rows of beads which move back and forth on wires or in grooves. Each bead had a value. Moving the beads to different positions helped the user to calculate sums.

Chores Girls helped their mother look after young children, wash dishes, bake bread, gather eggs from the henhouse, work in the garden, make clothes, and clean house. To keep dust down, girls sprinkled water on the floor. Floors were washed once a year. Boys helped their father herd livestock, gather and chop wood, clean the stable, and work in the fields. The government required all men and boys over 15 years to serve in the militia for one or two months each year.

manners, and how to read, write, and count. There were no classes in history, geography, or literature. Quill pens and ink wells were used to write, and all calculating was done with an abacus.

Boys and girls attended school in separate buildings. Some of the rules at girls' school at Notre Dame read: "They must be very modest in their clothing and their dress. They will not go bare-armed or with throat uncovered, nor curl their hair but keep it clean and neat. They must be dressed as simply as possible, without using more ribbons or bows than are absolutely necessary for tying their dress and sleeves."

The Jesuit priests taught the boys who wished to become priests. At the Jesuit school, pupils arose at 5:00 AM. On Thursdays, Sundays, and feast days, the pupils washed their faces. From 5:00 to 7:00 AM students said their prayers and studied Latin. Breakfast consisted of bread and water. Morning classes of Greek, religion, and philosophy were followed by study time until lunch at noon. Priests whipped the lazy and troublesome boys. Lunch was eaten in complete silence. After a short break came choir practice and then classes until 4:00 PM. The rest of the day consisted of play, supper, study, and prayers. By the time students went to bed at 9:00 PM, they had prayed for a total of three hours that day.

■ The Ursuline nuns were a very strict and devout female order of the Roman Catholic clergy. Their purpose was to educate and train the colony's young girls in the Catholic faith.

The Acadians: French Settlers of the COAST

The Acadians had a robust, but illegal, trade with New England.

New France was not the only French settlement to grow during this period. Although the settlement established by de Monts and Champlain at Port-Royal in 1605 had failed, French settlers returned to the area as early as 1610.

The French settlers called their new home "L'Acadie" or Acadia, and they were called Acadians. French settlement was interrupted for a few years while English and Scottish settlers claimed the area, renaming it Nova Scotia, which means "New Scotland." Then the French returned in 1632.

The Acadians settled along the Atlantic coast, where they hunted, fished, and farmed. The salt marshes along the shoreline had rich soil. To take advantage of this fertile soil for farming, the Acadians built dikes to keep out the water. They also caught fish by driving stakes into the river bottom at low tide to create a circular fence called a **weir**. At high tide the fish swam into the enclosure and became trapped as the tide receded. By 1650, the Acadians had stable agricultural production, and most families had adequate food and clothing.

The Acadians' diet consisted of pea soup, bread or porridge, salted beef and

FURTHER UNDERSTANDING

Dikes Dams or banks of earth are sometimes built as a protection against flooding. Acadians used a combination of logs and earth covered with sod to create a bank which was higher than the level of the water. A gate was constructed to control the flow of water into and out of the area.

■ The Acadians built a special type of dike that allowed overflowing seawater to drain off their farmland. The dikes kept many hectares of marshland dry enough to grow crops.

pork, mutton and fowl, maple syrup, herbs and garden vegetables, and fish and game. The men smoked tobacco, and the women chewed spruce gum, which helped digestion and cleansed the teeth. For goods they could not grow or manufacture, Acadians had a robust, but illegal, trade with New England.

A Pawn in European Wars

Life was not always peaceful for the Acadians. For much of the 1600s and 1700s, Britain and France were at war in Europe. These conflicts frequently spread to North America. Both European powers had claims to Acadia. France argued that Jacques Cartier had claimed Acadia for France. Britain maintained that John Cabot was the first European to claim Acadia.

Although Acadia had good agricultural land, the region was more important for its position near the Grand Banks, the best fishing grounds in North America. A British prime minister once declared he would rather lose his right arm than surrender these fisheries. A French politician claimed he would prefer to be stoned in the streets than lose the fisheries. Acadia was also a strategic military location at the entrance of the St. Lawrence River. Whoever controlled Acadia would be able to control the passage of ships up the St. Lawrence.

As a result of its military and commercial importance, Acadia was often fought over by France and Britain. In its first hundred years, Acadia changed hands nine times and was attacked by British troops ten other times. The Acadians did not want to fight for either the French or the British. They wished to be left alone, but history was not to allow it. Acadia was to play a critical role in the final resolution of French and English conflicts over North America.

■ Before fertile land could be farmed, French-Canadian settlers needed to clear the area of trees.

A Wealth of CULTURES

As New France developed, encounters between individuals and groups were inevitable. People learned about each other through their observations and interactions. They gained knowledge about North America and the people living there as a result of their experiences.

The excerpts below are quotations from written sources. They are believed to be the actual words of people from history. They reflect a variety of experiences and beliefs. It is important to remember that each quotation represents one person's thoughts at one point in time. Terms such as "barbarians" and "savages" reflect the language that was used at that time and the opinions of the speakers. Some terms used would not be considered appropriate today. Also, because there were few written histories or accounts by Aboriginal peoples of their first contact with Europeans, we are forced to rely on their impressions and reactions as they were reported by the French and to others.

ABORIGINAL PEOPLES AND MISSIONARIES

Jean de Brébeuf commented on the Hurons' resistance to the efforts of French missionaries to teach them European ways and the Roman Catholic religion:

... some of them are obstinate, and attached to their superstitions and evil customs. These are principally the old people; for beyond these, who are not numerous, the rest know nothing of their own belief. We have two or three of this number in our village. I am often in conflict with them; and when I show them they are wrong, and make them contradict themselves ... still they will not yield, always falling back upon this, that their Country is not like ours, that they have another God, another Paradise, in a word, other customs.

FRENCH MERCHANTS, SETTLERS, AND THE IROQUOIS

Merchant Pierre Boucher wrote about settlers' fears of the Iroquois:

Our enemies the Iroquois are preventing us from enjoying the commodities of the country ... We cannot go hunting, or fishing, for fear of being killed, or of being taken by these villains; and we cannot even plough our fields, or make hay, without continually putting ourselves at risk: for they throw up ambushes on every side and it only takes a single bush to shelter or rather conceal six or seven of these barbarians, who rush out at you any which way. So you can imagine that we are always on our guard and that a poor man is never safe for long if he wanders off from the others. A woman always worries that her husband, who departed in the morning to work, will be killed or captured, and that she will never see him again.

ABORIGINAL PEOPLES AND FRENCH EXPLORERS

La Vérendrye describes how he sought the help of a Cree man for his explorations:

... the man I have chosen is one named Auchagah, a savage of my post, greatly attached to the French nation, the man most capable of guiding a party, and with whom there would be no fear of our being abandoned on the way. When I proposed to him to guide me to the great river of the West he replied that he was at my service and would start whenever I wished.

GOVERNMENT OFFICIALS AND ILLEGAL FUR TRADERS

Intendant Jacques Duchesneau commented about his frustration with illegal fur trading:

I ruled against the coureurs de bois, against the merchants who provide them with goods. All that has been useless because several powerful families of the country are deeply involved and the governor lets them do it and even shares in the profits with them.

THE HURON AND "STRANGERS"

In *Jesuit Relations*, Brébeuf recorded his impression of the Hurons' ready acceptance of "strangers":

Their hospitality towards all sorts of strangers is remarkable; they present to them in their feasts, the best of what they have prepared, and, as I have already said, I do not know if anything similar, in this regard, is to be found anywhere. They never close the door upon a stranger, and, once having received him into their houses, they share with him the best they have; they never send him away, and when he goes away of his own accord, he repays them by a simple "thank you."

ENGLISH FUR TRADERS AND ABORIGINAL PEOPLES

Andrew Graham worked as chief factor at York Factory in the late 1700s. He describes a meeting between the leaders of an Aboriginal trading party, called trading captains, and representatives of the Hudson's Bay Company:

Chairs are placed in the room, and pipes with smoking materials produced on the table. The captains place themselves on each side of the Governor... The silence is then broken by degrees by the most venerable Indian [that is, the one most deserving of respect] ... He tells how many canoes he has brought, what kind of winter they have had, what natives he has seen, are coming, or stay behind, asks how the Englishmen do, and says he is glad to see them. After which the Governor bids him welcome, tells them he has good goods and plenty; and that he loves the Indians and will be kind to them.

NUNS AND FAMILIES

In 1665, Marie de l'Incarnation wrote about her observations of the families in New France:

There are many poor people here and the reason is that when a family creates a household, it takes two or three years before they have enough to eat, not to mention enough clothing, furniture and a whole range of little things needed for the upkeep of a household; but once these hardships are behind them, they start to feel more comfortable, and if they conduct themselves well, then they become rich over time, as much as a new country like this will allow.

Multiple Choice

Choose the best answer in the multiple choice questions that follow.

1 Who was the first French missionary to come to Canada?
a) Father Jean de Brébeuf
b) Father Chrétien Le Clercq
c) Father Abbé Jessé Fléché
d) Saint Joseph

2 What were the *Jesuit Relations*?
a) the name of the missions established in New France
b) reports written by missionaries describing their experiences in New France
c) an instructional manual for the Jesuits working in New France
d) the name of the boats used by the Jesuits to reach Canada

3 Who was granted control of the fur trade in 1627, in exchange for a promise to settle 4,000 Roman Catholics along the St. Lawrence within fifteen years?
a) The Company of One Hundred Associates
b) The Hudson's Bay Company
c) Jean-Baptiste Colbert
d) The North West Company

4 Who were the voyageurs?
a) travelling priests
b) french fur traders
c) settlers from France
d) Aboriginal fur traders

5 Which fur trader and explorer built a post at Lake of the Woods in 1732?
a) Henry Kelsey
b) Alexander Mackenzie
c) Peter Pond
d) Pierre de La Vérendrye

6 Which of the following was not a duty of a seigneur?
a) granting land to settlers
b) reporting on the crops to the intendant
c) creating a police force to patrol the countryside
d) building a flour mill for the habitants

7 Which of the following was not a responsibility of the habitants?
a) volunteer once a year with the fire brigade
b) work a few days each year on the seigneur's land
c) give the seigneur one-tenth of all the fish caught each year
d) pay a tax if land was sold outside the family

8 At what age were children in New France expected to begin helping with the chores?
a) 5 years old
b) 6 years old
c) 7 years old
d) 8 years old

Mix and Match

Match the description in column A with the correct terms in column B. There are more terms than descriptions.

A

1. The Black Robes
2. Orphans raised at the expense of the government of France and later sent to New France
3. A Récollet missionary who was the first European to notice that the Mi'kmaq had their own form of writing
4. Founder of the Jesuit mission in Huronia
5. Religious order of the Roman Catholic Church that established the first school in New France
6. First intendant of New France
7. Joined the Hudson's Bay Company as a clerk at the age of 17

B

a) Ursuline nuns
b) Jean de Brébeuf
c) Jesuits
d) Jean Talon
e) Seigneurs
f) Father Chrétien Le Clercq
g) *les filles du roi*
h) Jean-Baptiste Colbert
i) Henry Kelsey

Time Line

Find the appropriate spot on the time line for each event listed below.

A Beginning of the Seven Years' War

B The first Ursuline nuns arrive in New France

C The population of New France has increased to more than 9,000 European settlers

D Father Jean de Brébeuf founds the first Jesuit mission in Huronia

E End of the fur trade wars

F The Huron nation is destroyed

1603 – Samuel de Champlain makes his first trip to New France
1609 – Champlain joins the Huron and their allies in a battle against the Iroquois
1626 **1**
1627 – Fewer than 100 European settlers live in New France
1635 – Champlain dies
1639 **2**

1642 – Paul de Chomedey and fifty other settlers found Ville-Marie, the future site of Montréal
1649 – Father Brébeuf is killed during an Iroquois attack
1650 **3**
1665 – King Louis XIV sends 1,200 soldiers to New France
1670 – The Hudson's Bay Company is formed

1673 – Louis Jolliet and Father Jacques Marquette find the Mississippi River
1674 – François de Laval is appointed the first bishop of New France
1679 **4**
1690 **5**
1756 **6**

Conclusion

Many individuals and groups contributed to the development of New France and the fur trade. Participants included Aboriginal peoples, European monarchs, French explorers, Jesuits, nuns, seigneurs, habitants and other settlers, French and English fur traders, and appointed officials.

Establishing New France was a struggle at times. Unfamiliar environmental conditions and vast lands made exploration and settlement a challenge. Conflicts between nations and groups further complicated matters. England and France both wanted to claim the area and advance their empires. Aboriginal groups helped in the fur trade, but their associations with European allies led to their involvement in the fur-trade wars.

The king of France and his appointed officials had to work to ensure the population of New France would increase. *Les filles du roi* and other settlers were encouraged to move to New France with incentives such as money and land. Eventually, New France prospered and Acadia grew. However, the long-standing conflict between Britain and France was not over. New conflicts would arise as the two continued to struggle against each other for control of North America.

Further Information

Suggested Reading

Greer, Allan. *People of New France*. Toronto: University of Toronto Press, 1997.

Innis, Harold A. *The Fur Trade in Canada*. Toronto: University of Toronto Press, 1999.

Nelson, George, Laura Peers and Theresa Schenk (ed.). *My First Years in The Fur Trade: The Journals Of 1802–1804*. Montréal: McGill-Queen's University Press, 2002.

Sioui, Georges E. *Huron-Wendat: The Heritage of the Circle*. Vancouver: UBC Press, 1999.

Internet Resources

Canada: A People's History Online
history.cbc.ca
The online companion to CBC's award-winning television series on the history of Canada, as told through the eyes of its people. This multi-media Web site features behind-the-scenes information, games and puzzles, and discussion boards. Also available in French.

Exploration, the Fur Trade, and Hudson's Bay Company
www.canadiana.org/hbc
This Web site specializes in early Canadian history. Special features include a time line, stories, and personalities. Articles are available in both French and English.

Glossary

baptized: dipped into or washed with water; Christians believe this act purifies a person from sin and admits them into the faith

charter: a grant from a government or company permitting the formation of an organization with certain privileges

Christianity: a religion based upon the life and teachings of Jesus Christ

clergy: a group or body of people trained to perform religious services

colony: a settlement created by people who have left their own country to settle in another land

commander-in-chief: the person who has complete command of a country's armed forces

Continental Divide: an imaginary line along the Rocky Mountains that separates those rivers that flow west to the Pacific Ocean and those that flow east to the Atlantic Ocean

livres: a type of money formerly used in France; one livre was worth a pound of silver

mission: a religious headquarters in a foreign country

monopoly: guaranteed control of a service or market without competition; granted by the government

peasants: farmers who rent their lands or work the farm for its owner

raw materials: materials that will be manufactured into something else

smallpox: a highly infectious and often fatal disease; characterized by high fever and pimples that blister

weir: large trap or fence made of branches or wooden poles placed across a stream to catch fish; once the fish were trapped, they could be speared more easily

Answers

Multiple Choice	Mix and Match	Time Line
1. c)	1. c)	1. d)
2. b)	2. g)	2. b)
3. a)	3. f)	3. f)
4. b)	4. b)	4. c)
5. d)	5. a)	5. e)
6. c)	6. d)	6. a)
7. a)	7. i)	
8. c)		

Index